POCKET PRAYERS
FOR
COMMUTERS

POCKET PRAYERS FOR COMMUTERS

COMPILED BY
CHRISTOPHER HERBERT

CHURCH HOUSE
PUBLISHING

Church House Publishing
Church House
Great Smith Street
London SW1P 3AZ

ISBN 978 0 7151 4194 6

Published 2009 by Church House Publishing

Designed by www.penguinboy.net
Printed in England by Ashford Colour Press Ltd, Fareham, Hants

CONTENTS

INTRODUCTION

If you left home this morning to commute to work, the chances are that you will have had a range of experiences. Your thoughts and emotions, your worries and your delights will all have been jostling against each other on your way to the station. Perhaps you were running late or maybe (maybe?) there was nowhere to park or it might have been dark, wet and miserable. Then, on the train, the carriage was, as usual, packed. It's not exactly a stress-free or easy way to begin the day, is it?

And in case all this is not enough to contend with, you may also be worrying about a situation in your own family or about a difficulty you face at work.

And then, after you have faced whatever work holds for you today, there will be the journey back home to contend with – the crowds out in the street hurrying, heads down, eager to get to the station or the bus. The subdued hubbub in the station concourse, and then an infuriatingly unruffled and disembodied voice saying, 'We apologise for the late arrival of . . .'

It's a turbulent way to live and, as a result, some of the things that might give you a moment of peace or a time for reflection are crowded out. The very notion of a work-life balance causes you to smile wryly or even cynically . . .

But suppose that inside all the things you are experiencing, real peace is waiting to be found? Peace of mind, peace of soul. Put it another way, suppose that God himself is actually present with you, waiting to be discovered; the still, small voice hidden inside all the turbulence that you and your fellow-commuters face each day?

It is not a fanciful thought. There is plenty of evidence in the Bible, and in the lives of Christians, that people under stress have found that God really is present with them, even in the most demanding or the unlikeliest circumstances.

This book is designed to help you structure some of your thoughts by offering you a pattern of ideas around which you can pray. Prayer and thinking are closely aligned activities. In prayer, you are doing your thinking in the presence of God and directing your attention towards the Almighty. You are making space and time to take your mind and soul on a walk towards God and the world. The prayers and reflections are meant to help you to 'walk' at a certain pace, slowly and thoughtfully. There should be no rush and certainly there are no deadlines to meet.

Each day there are prayers and readings for the journey to work and for the journey homewards. They follow a number of themes and the mornings and evenings echo each other.

It is my hope that this small book will help you to walk closer with God and discover the delights and challenges of doing so.

ON THE WAY TO WORK: MORNING PRAYER

PRESENCE AND PEACE

Prayer is bringing yourself, your concerns and everyone you love into the presence of God who is love, knowing that he is with you now and always. So each session begins with a time when you place yourself consciously in the presence of God. Of course, God is with us at every moment. He is as close and as intimate to us as breathing, but in prayer we bring all that to mind.

Let the words of the opening sentence or prayer act like the hands of a potter making a pot: allow the words to mould your thinking and praying. Say the words to yourself slowly, a few times, and then wait; that's all, just wait. What you are doing is bringing your very self into the presence of God. It may take the whole journey just to do that. And if it does, so be it.

PRAISE

Once you feel you have some kind of inner peace, if only for a brief moment, you could turn to the prayer or passage of Scripture inviting you to offer praise. God is always very close to us, waiting for our response of love, and this is a moment to call to mind not only being in God's presence but also the pleasure of being with him.

READING AND REFLECTION

Each day in the pages that follow you will find a biblical passage for you to think about. There are a number of suggestions to help you to read the passage thoughtfully, but you may want to ignore those suggestions and approach the text in your own way. That's fine, but please let both your imagination and your intelligence play their part in what you are doing. And again, don't rush. Reading the Scriptures as a part of prayer needs to be done with an open mind and with gentle, rigorous patience.

PRAYER

Now begin to turn towards all those people or situations that are on your own heart. Think of the people you are going to meet later today: a colleague, a friend, a stranger – perhaps the people who are sitting around you on the bus or train. Imagine that they are with you now and accompany them into the presence of God. Ask God to bless them and to look upon them with love.

And finally, pray for anyone you have had to leave at home today; with them and for them, in silence, say: 'Our Father . . .'

CONCLUSION

At the end of the 'Our Father' there is a closing prayer to send you out into the day that lies ahead. You might want to try to memorise and hold on to a phrase from this – or from any part of the session – to repeat to yourself throughout the day.

THE JOURNEY HOME: EVENING PRAYER

On the journey homewards, hopefully there comes a moment where the cares of the workaday world begin to be shed and in their stead new, home-directed thoughts and issues take over. Some of those home-concerns may be of enormous and worrying importance, others much more mundane, but sometimes, deeper still, there are more profound moments of introspection about life and its meaning.

There will also come a point, perhaps on the journey itself or, perhaps, later in the evening, when time can be found to reflect on the day that has passed. It's a sort of tidying-up-and-putting-to-one-side kind of process, a time for turning down the lights and for placing all that has happened before God.

The structure for Evening Prayer is similar to that for Morning Prayer, but with some variations appropriate to the time of day and the different mood of journeying home.

PRESENCE AND PEACE

As with Morning Prayer, this is a moment to focus on God, and to try to achieve a sense of stillness and peace in his presence amongst the commotion of the journey. It will be easier if you have managed to get a seat – but by no means impossible if you haven't!

READING

As with Morning Prayer, the Bible readings have been selected because they represent some of the most powerful and important elements of our faith. In fact, the readings in the evening sessions echo the readings from the Morning Prayer time.

The readings are followed by Reflections designed to help you to think about one or more of the themes of the reading. At night especially, it is important not to struggle intellectually with each reading, that's for the daytime. In the evening, the mode and the mood are different. They should be marked by a kind of willing and restful patience.

CONFESSION

The reflections will almost inevitably prompt more serious thought about what has happened during the day, and any things that have left you uneasy or with a troubled conscience. You can, if you wish, examine your soul by asking some questions about your own attitudes, thoughts and behaviour.

The fact is, as human beings we are extraordinarily adept at deceiving ourselves, and therefore, from time to time, in an act of confession before God, we need to be absolutely honest with ourselves and with God. We need to acknowledge what we are truly like and ask God to help us to amend our ways and to become the people he would have us be. Do not wallow in your time of confession; that's a form of self-indulgence. Once you have confessed to God, move on. Think not of yourself but of others.

PRAYER

Offer prayers of thanksgiving for the day that has
passed. If there are things that concern you, place
those also in God's hands. Chew over them for a while
if you like, but try not to worry over them like a dog
worrying a bone. God knows you and your concerns
and looks on you with love. And then, finally, as an act
of trust say: 'Our Father'.

CONCLUSION

Then, simply hand yourself over to God. Leave your
thoughts, your worries and the day that has passed
with him, knowing that his redeeming and healing love
are always at work, reconciling all things to himself.

THE LORD'S PRAYER

Our Father in heaven,
hallowed be your name,
your kingdom come,
your will be done,
on earth as in heaven.
Give us today our daily bread.
Forgive us our sins
as we forgive those who sin against us.
Lead us not into temptation
but deliver us from evil.
For the kingdom, the power,
and the glory are yours
now and for ever.
Amen.

Week
one

MONDAY MORNING

PRESENCE AND PEACE Psalm 27.17

Wait for the Lord;
be strong and he shall comfort your heart;
wait patiently for the Lord.

Still my heart, O Lord, still my heart that I may come into your presence in peace.

PRAISE

Glory to the Father and to the Son and to the Holy Spirit, as it was in the beginning, is now and shall be for ever. Amen.

READING 1 Kings 19.11-12

[The word of the Lord came to Elijah:] 'Go and stand on the mount before the Lord.' The Lord was passing by: a great and strong wind came, rending mountains and shattering rocks before him, but the Lord was not in the wind; and after the wind there was an earthquake, but the Lord was not in the earthquake; and after the earthquake fire, but the Lord was not in the fire; and after the fire a faint murmuring sound . . .

REFLECTION

*This story represents one of the great turning points in the
history of human thinking. God was not to be found in power
but revealed himself very humbly, in a 'faint murmuring
sound'. Or, in the Authorized Version of the Bible, 'a still, small
voice . . .' While there can be no doubt of God's immense
power, nevertheless it has been the Christian experience that
God reveals himself in quietness and humility.*

*Do your ideas about God include his courteous humility as
well as his power?*

PRAYER

*Think of the people you are going to be meeting later today: a
colleague, a stranger or a friend. Bring them with you into the
presence of God. Ask God to bless them and to look upon
them with love.*

*Think of some experience you have already had today for
which you would like to give thanks to God.*

Our Father . . .

CONCLUSION

Father, this day is yours; may the peace you have granted
me rest in my heart now and for ever. Amen.

MONDAY EVENING

PRESENCE AND PEACE Romans 11.33,36
How deep are the wealth and the wisdom and the
knowledge of God!
From him and through him and for him all things exist.

READING Exodus 3.2,4-6,13-14
There an angel of the Lord appeared to him as a fire
blazing out from a bush. Although the bush was on fire,
it was not being burnt up ... When the Lord saw that
Moses had turned aside to look, he called to him out of
the bush, 'Moses, Moses!' He answered, 'Here I am!' God
said, 'Do not come near! Take off your sandals, for the
place where you are standing is holy ground.' Then he
said 'I am the God of your father, the God of Abraham,
Isaac, and Jacob.' Moses hid his face, for he was afraid to
look at God ...

Moses said to God, 'If I come to the Israelites and tell
them that the God of their forefathers has sent me to
them, and they ask me his name, what am I to say to
them?' God answered, 'I AM that I am. Tell them that I
AM has sent you to them.'

REFLECTION

This is another of those great turning points in the history of our human understanding of God. God is not small or locked into tribal boundaries; he is 'I AM', the One Who Is. The simplicity and the profundity of this insight are breathtaking. As you are at prayer so your very self (your own 'I am') is deeply related to the 'I AM' of God's self. It's as though your heart and the heart of God are pulsing together in harmony. God's 'I AM' holds your 'I am' in being.

CONFESSION

Lord, have mercy upon us,
Christ, have mercy upon us,
Lord, have mercy upon us.

PRAYER

Thank God for the gift of prayer. Pray that God will help you to develop and enrich your relationship with him. Place into the hands of God all the things that have delighted you or troubled you this day and ask him to surround all those things with his healing love.

Our Father . . .

CONCLUSION

The grace of our Lord Jesus Christ and the love of God and the fellowship of the Holy Spirit be with us all evermore. Amen.

TUESDAY MORNING

PRESENCE AND PEACE 1 Samuel 2.2

There is none but you,
none so holy as the Lord,
none so righteous as our God.

I come into your holy presence, O Lord;
look upon me with mercy and love.

PRAISE Luke 1.46-47

My soul tells out the greatness of the Lord,
my spirit has rejoiced in God my Saviour.

READING Luke 1.26-32,34-35,38

In the sixth month the angel Gabriel was sent by God to
Nazareth, a town in Galilee, with a message for a girl
betrothed to a man named Joseph; a descendant of
David; the girl's name was Mary. The angel went in and
said to her, 'Greetings, most favoured one! The Lord is
with you.' But she was deeply troubled by what he said
and wondered what this greeting could mean. Then the
angel said to her, 'Do not be afraid, Mary, for God has
been gracious to you; you will conceive and give birth to
a son, and you are to give him the name Jesus. He will be

great, and will be called Son of the Most High.' . . . 'How can this be?' said Mary, 'I am still a virgin.' The angel answered, 'The Holy Spirit will come upon you, and the power of the Most High will overshadow you' . . . 'I am the Lord's servant,' said Mary; 'may it be as you have said.' Then the angel left her.

REFLECTION
Picture the scene: Mary in her room, the early morning sunlight streaming through the window. In that light, shimmering with promise and beauty, she sees an angel, a messenger from God. It is an encounter that will change the world.

PRAYER
Give thanks for Mary's 'Yes' to the light of Christ. Look at the daylight and imagine that it has come streaming from the throne of God. As it enters your eyes, so let the joy of God enter your soul. Thank God for the daylight. Pray for those who live in a kind of inner, angry darkness and who are in turmoil.

Our Father . . .

CONCLUSION
Lord, as the light bathes the earth with its beauty, may your light shine upon all whom I shall meet this day.

TUESDAY EVENING

PRESENCE AND PEACE Daniel 2.20-21
Blessed be God's name from age to age,
for to him belong wisdom and power.
He changes seasons and times;
he deposes kings and sets up kings;
he gives wisdom to the wise
and knowledge to those who have discernment.

READING Hosea 6.1-3
Come, let us return to the Lord.
He has torn us, but he will heal us,
he has wounded us, but he will bind up our wounds;
after two days he will revive us,
on the third day he will raise us
to live in his presence.
Let us strive to know the Lord,
whose coming is as sure as the sunrise.
He will come to us like the rain,
like spring rains that water the earth.

REFLECTION

It was the experience of the Chosen People that, in spite of their faults and failings, God took the initiative to redeem them. His love would never let them go. New life always rebuilt the citadel of their lives.

What is there in your own life that needs to be reshaped or renewed by God?

CONFESSION

Holy God,
holy and strong,
holy and immortal,
have mercy upon us.

PRAYER

Thank God for the new things you have learned this day and for new opportunities that seem to beckon.
Pray for those writers, actors and musicians whose work has brought you new insights.

Our Father . . .

CONCLUSION

May the Lord bless us,
may he keep us from all evil
and lead us to the glory of life everlasting. Amen.

WEDNESDAY MORNING

PRESENCE AND PEACE

Lord, let your light pour into my heart,
that I may praise you with my whole being,
for Jesus' sake. Amen.

PRAISE Psalm 27.1

The Lord is my light and my salvation;
  whom then shall I fear?
The Lord is the strength of my life;
  of whom then shall I be afraid?

READING Luke 1.39-45

Soon afterwards Mary set out and hurried away to a town in the uplands of Judah. She went into Zechariah's house and greeted Elizabeth. And when Elizabeth heard Mary's greeting, the baby stirred in her womb. Then Elizabeth was filled with the Holy Spirit and exclaimed in a loud voice, 'God's blessing is on you above all women, and his blessing is on the fruit of your womb. Who am I, that the mother of my Lord should visit me? I tell you, when your greeting sounded in my ears, the baby in my womb leapt for joy. Happy is she who has had faith that the Lord's promise to her would be fulfilled!'

REFLECTION

Imagine that moment when Mary and Elizabeth met; two women from the same extended family, both expecting babies. You can see the joy in their eyes, the sheer wonder in the way they smile at each other and then embrace.

Just as Mary hastened to visit Elizabeth, so God hastens to us. And what is our response?

PRAYER

Pray for all who are expecting babies.
Pray for the fathers and mothers you know.

Our Father . . .

CONCLUSION

Creator God, we give you thanks for the unutterable joy and miracle of all new life.

. . . in the tender compassion of our God,
the dawn from heaven will break upon us,
to shine on those who live in darkness,
under the shadow of death,
and to guide our feet into the way of peace.
Luke 1.78-79

WEDNESDAY EVENING

PRESENCE AND PEACE Psalm 9.10
And those who know your name
will put their trust in you,
for you, Lord, have never failed those who seek you.

READING Genesis 21.1-3,6-7
The Lord showed favour to Sarah as he had promised,
and made good what he had said about her. She
conceived and at the time foretold by God she bore a
son to Abraham in his old age. The son whom Sarah bore
to him Abraham named Isaac . . . Sarah said, 'God has
given me good reason to laugh, and everyone who hears
will laugh with me.' She added, 'Whoever would have
told Abraham that Sarah would suckle children? Yet I
have borne him a son in his old age.'

REFLECTION
*In this episode in the life of Abraham and Sarah we are given
a glimpse of that delight that frequently accompanies the
arrival of a baby. Everything seems so full of promise;
everything seems to reflect the joyous light of eternity. The
birth of a child is a glory, a miracle, a song that whispers its
own alleluia.*

Think back over your own life, and give thanks for any moments of joy that have been so wonderful, you cannot put them into words.

CONFESSION

Almighty God, when we fail to see you in moments of joy, forgive our blindness and arrogance of heart, for Jesus' sake. Amen.

PRAYER

Thank God for those things that have happened this day which have brought laughter to your eyes.
Pray for all those children in the world whose lives are marked and maimed by poverty and disease.
Pray for those who work in health care, especially your own doctor.

Our Father . . .

CONCLUSION

God be in my head and in my understanding;
God be in my eyes and in my looking;
God be in my mouth and in my speaking;
God be at my end and at my departing.
Richard Pynson (1448–1529)

THURSDAY MORNING

PRESENCE AND PEACE Isaiah 49.13

Shout for joy, you heavens; earth, rejoice;
break into songs of triumph, you mountains,
for the Lord has comforted his people
and has had pity on them in their distress.

May the songs of heaven be within me and around me
this day and always.

PRAISE Luke 1.68-69

Praise to the Lord, the God of Israel!
For he has turned to his people and set them free.
He has raised for us a strong deliverer
from the house of his servant David.

READING Luke 1.57,59-64

When the time came for Elizabeth's child to be born, she
gave birth to a son . . . On the eighth day they came to
circumcise the child; and they were going to name him
Zechariah after his father, but his mother spoke up: 'No!'
she said. 'He is to be called John.' 'But', they said, 'there is
nobody in your family who has that name.' They
enquired of his father by signs what he would like him to

be called. He asked for a writing tablet and to everybody's astonishment wrote, 'His name is John.' Immediately his lips and tongue were freed and he began to speak, praising God.

REFLECTION

There is, in this story of Zechariah, a palpable sense of release. Zechariah is released from his inability to speak but ironically the people standing around are dumbfounded. Once they have recovered from the shock they ask what the future of the child will be. Liberation and release are great gifts. They open us up to new possibilities. What are those things that leave you in a kind of imprisoned speechlessness? What needs to happen to help you to face the future?

PRAYER

Pray for any people you know who are deeply unhappy, that they may rediscover a joy they once knew.
Pray for those who face this day in real distress of mind or body, that they may experience God's strength upon them.

Our Father . . .

CONCLUSION

Father in heaven, I commend myself into your loving hands this day; may your Spirit be within me so that my life may be a song of praise for you, now and for ever.

THURSDAY EVENING

PRESENCE AND PEACE Psalm 63.1

O God, you are my God; eagerly I seek you;
my soul is athirst for you

READING Exodus 2.5-8,10

Pharaoh's daughter came down to bathe in the river,
while her ladies-in-waiting walked on the bank. She
noticed the basket among the reeds and sent her slave-
girl to bring it. When she opened it, there was the baby;
it was crying, and she was moved with pity for it. 'This
must be one of the Hebrew children,' she said. At this
the sister approached Pharaoh's daughter: 'Shall I go and
fetch you one of the Hebrew women to act as a wet-
nurse for the child?' When Pharaoh's daughter told her
to do so, she went and called the baby's mother . . . She
took the child and nursed him at her breast. Then, when
he was old enough, she brought him to Pharaoh's
daughter, who adopted him and called him Moses,
'because', said she, 'I drew him out of the water.'

REFLECTION

*In the Bible, the act of naming has great significance. In your
reflection this evening think about what it means for God to*

know your name. He knows you deeply and, with affection,
addresses you as you are.

CONFESSION

Almighty God,
to whom all hearts are open,
all desires known,
and from whom no secrets are hidden,
cleanse the thoughts of our hearts
by the inspiration of your Holy Spirit,
that we may perfectly love you, and worthily magnify
your holy name,
through Christ our lord.
Amen.

Prayer of Preparation, Common Worship

PRAYER

Thank God for the day that has passed and for those people
whose names you have come to know.

Our Father . . .

CONCLUSION

Father, you have called me by name; by your Holy Spirit
help me to deepen my love for you and for others; for
Jesus' sake.

FRIDAY MORNING

PRESENCE AND PEACE Psalm 40.12
Do not withhold your compassion from me, O Lord;
let your love and your faithfulness always preserve me.

Lord, your tender care surrounds me; lead me this day in
the paths of truth and love.

PRAISE Isaiah 9.2
The people that walked in darkness
have seen a great light;
on those who lived in a land as dark as death
a light has dawned.

Lord of the light, we praise you for your great beauty.

READING Luke 2.1; 4-7
In those days a decree was issued by the emperor
Augustus for a census to be taken throughout the
Roman world . . . Joseph went up to Judaea from the
town of Nazareth in Galilee, to register in the city of
David called Bethlehem, because he was of the house of
David by descent; and with him went Mary, his
betrothed, who was expecting her child. While they

were there the time came for her to have her baby, and she gave birth to a son, her firstborn. She wrapped him in swaddling clothes, and laid him in a manger, because there was no room for them at the inn.

REFLECTION

This story is told by Luke so simply and yet it is a story that has captured the imagination of the world. A young woman gives birth to a child, who is the Son of God, in a stable. The eternal becomes subject to time; the infinite is revealed in the tiny details of a baby's face; the love and truth that hold all things in being are held in the encircling arms of Mary. Is it any wonder that poets and artists across the centuries have tried to explore the paradoxes and beauties in this most holy story? Imagine Mary holding the baby; what are the truths that you will face this day that will need to be held in a tender, strong embrace?

PRAYER

Thank God for the power of the revelation of himself in the child, Jesus.
Pray for all parents you know who may sometimes feel overwhelmed by the responsibilities of care.

Our Father . . .

CONCLUSION

Father God, I trust you, through Jesus Christ my Lord.

FRIDAY EVENING

PRESENCE AND PEACE Psalm 7.10
God is my shield that is over me;
he saves the true of heart.

READING Isaiah 49.14-16
But Zion says,
'The Lord has forsaken me;
my Lord has forgotten me.'
Can a woman forget the infant at her breast,
or a mother the child of her womb?
But should even these forget,
I shall never forget you.
I have inscribed you on the palms of my hands;
your walls are always before my eyes.

REFLECTION
*One of the most powerful images of human love and
sacrificial compassion is a mother cradling her newborn child.
The relationship of God with his people is very like that, and
yet there are times when we forget or deny it. In the passage
from Isaiah the author speaks about God being in an even
closer relationship with his people than a mother with her
child.*

If God is as close to us as that, there is nowhere we can go that is beyond his mercy and loving-kindness. Allow this truth to shape your thinking and your behaviour.

CONFESSION

Lord, for your tender mercy's sake, lay not our sins to our charge but forgive what is past and give us grace to amend our sinful lives; to decline from sin and incline to virtue, that we may walk with a perfect heart before you, now and evermore.

Bishop Ridley's Prayers (1566)

PRAYER

Give thanks for those people you have met this day, who by their lives and actions have reflected something of the nature of God. Pray for those who face this coming night in any kind of anguish or loneliness. Pray for all those who are in prison and for those who work in the prison service.

Our Father . . .

CONCLUSION

Blessed be the God and Father of our Lord Jesus Christ, who has conferred on us in Christ every spiritual blessing in the heavenly realms.

Ephesians 1.3

WEEK
TWO

MONDAY MORNING

PRESENCE AND PEACE Psalm 145.19
The Lord is near to those who call upon him,
to all who call upon him faithfully.

Lord, from the depths of my heart I call to you;
be with me in all I think or say or do this day, for Jesus'
sake. Amen.

PRAISE Psalm145.10-11
All your works praise you, O Lord,
and your faithful servants bless you.
They tell of the glory of your kingdom
and speak of your mighty power.

READING Luke 2.8-14
Now in this same district there were shepherds out in
the fields, keeping watch through the night over their
flock. Suddenly an angel of the Lord appeared to them,
and the glory of the Lord shone round them. They were
terrified, but the angel said, 'Do not be afraid; I bring you
good news, news of great joy for the whole nation.
Today there has been born to you in the city of David a
deliverer – the Messiah, the Lord. This will be the sign for

24

you: you will find a baby wrapped in swaddling clothes, and lying in a manger.' All at once there was with the angel a great company of the heavenly host, singing praise to God: 'Glory to God in highest heaven, and on earth peace to all in whom he delights.'

REFLECTION

From that hill outside Bethlehem, the shepherds saw the skies become tumultuous with glory . . . Somehow the simplicity with which Luke tells this story gets under our guard, and we find ourselves entering the wonder of it all.

Some mysteries we explore not by staying outside them, but by entering them and seeing where they lead.

PRAYER

Pray for all those people who find it hard to enter mystery and who keep the wonder of things at arm's length.
Pray for yourself, that this day may be one in which shafts of glory are allowed to pierce the mundane.

Our Father . . .

CONCLUSION

Father in heaven, open my eyes, open my mind and open my soul to the mystery of life, in Jesus Christ our Lord. Amen.

MONDAY EVENING

PRESENCE AND PEACE Psalm 145.3
Great is the Lord and highly to be praised;
his greatness is beyond all searching out.

Allow yourself to rest in the holy mystery and presence
of God, and wait . . .

READING Isaiah 6.1-3
In the year that King Uzziah died I saw the Lord seated
on a throne, high and exalted, and the skirt of his robe
filled the temple. Seraphim were in attendance on him.
Each had six wings: with one pair of wings they covered
their faces and with another their bodies, and with the
third pair they flew. They were calling to one another,
    'Holy, holy, holy is the Lord of Hosts:
    the whole earth is full of his glory.'

REFLECTION
It is sometimes very difficult to find words or images that are
adequate to describe God's majesty, power and otherness.
Whether this image is one that appeals to you or not, there
are times when the absolute otherness and holiness of God
become of great importance, particularly when sentimentality

*and a kind of overfamiliarity are in the ascendant. In the life
of prayer there are moments, and sometimes seasons, when
God's glory is beyond all understanding, and prayer stutters
into an awed silence. If and when that happens all that we can
do is to wait faithfully in the silence, trusting that God's
self-revelation will break through in due course.*

CONFESSION

Most holy and most merciful God, look upon our sins
and weakness with compassion, and lead us, we pray,
with bonds of love, into the glory of your presence,
where all that separates us from you will be overcome,
through the death and resurrection of Jesus Christ our
Saviour and mighty Redeemer. Amen.

PRAYER

*Give thanks that God is God . . .
Pray for those who have no fear of God before their eyes.
Pray for yourself that God may be known in times of closeness
and in times of desolation.*

Our Father . . .

CONCLUSION

Into your merciful care and keeping O God, I commit
myself and all whom I love, this night and for evermore,
through Jesus Christ our Lord. Amen.

TUESDAY MORNING

PRESENCE AND PEACE Psalm 36.9
'. . . with you is the well of life,
and in your light shall we see light.'

PRAISE Psalm 89.1
My song shall be always
of the loving-kindness of the Lord:
with my mouth will I proclaim your faithfulness
throughout all generations.

READING Luke 2.28-35
 [Simeon took the child Jesus] in his arms, praised God,
and said:
Now, Lord, you are releasing your servant in peace,
according to your promise.
For I have seen with my own eyes
the deliverance you have made ready in full view
of all nations:
a light that will bring revelation to the Gentiles
and glory to your people Israel.'
The child's father and mother were full of wonder at
what was being said about him. Simeon blessed them and
said to Mary his mother, 'This child is destined to be a

sign that will be rejected; and you too will be pierced to the heart. Many in Israel will stand or fall because of him; and so the secret thoughts of many will be laid bare.'

REFLECTION

This beautiful story from Luke rests on the poignant contrast between a life coming to its end and the new life of a baby. But it is a story that, for all its beauty, has within it a threat of darkness. There is talk of Mary's own forthcoming sorrow and anguish, a prophecy that was to become a terrible reality at the crucifixion. To believe in Christ is not to become protected from sorrow or grief. Both are part of the human condition. What is true for a believer, however, is that no darkness can overtake us that is beyond the power of God to redeem.

PRAYER

Pray that, if the darkness engulfs you, you will discover God very near.
Pray for all those who are old, that they may be aware of the promise of God in Jesus Christ, and for those working in care and nursing homes for the elderly.

Our Father . . .

CONCLUSION

Holy and merciful God, be with me in my sorrows and in my joys, that my life may be made whole through your love, in Jesus Christ our Lord.

TUESDAY EVENING

PRESENCE AND PEACE Psalm 3.3
. . . you, Lord, are a shield about me;
you are my glory, and the lifter up of my head.

READING Genesis 17.1-5
When Abram was ninety-nine years old, the Lord
appeared to him and said, 'I am God Almighty. Live
always in my presence and be blameless, so that I may
make my covenant with you and give you many
descendants.' Abram bowed low, and God went on, 'This
is my covenant with you: you are to be the father of
many nations. Your name will no longer be Abram, but
Abraham; for I shall make you father of many nations.'

REFLECTION
*The Bible shows that God makes covenants with his people,
that is, solemn and unbreakable promises of solidarity, care
and hope. God calls Abraham from his home in Haran and
leads him into a new land. Even though Abraham is
apparently a very old man, God chooses him and promises
that he will be the father of many nations.*

For Christians, the covenant that God makes with Abraham is extended and renewed in the life, death and resurrection of Jesus Christ. As his followers, we are enfolded in the new and unbreakable promises of God. What does it mean to you to be enfolded in such a way?

CONFESSION

O God of unbreakable love, when I spurn and damage your covenant, have mercy upon me, forgive me all my sins, and turn me to walk in the right way, through Jesus Christ our Lord, Amen.

PRAYER

God made me.
God loves me and keeps me,
gives comfort and grace
for every need
at every moment
on and around me
within me. Thanks be to God.
George Appleton (1902–93)

Our Father . . .

CONCLUSION

Holy God, look upon me, and all whom I love, with eyes of infinite compassion, and let us rest our souls in you, this night and for evermore. Amen.

WEDNESDAY MORNING

PRESENCE AND PEACE Psalm 40.1

I waited patiently for the Lord;
he inclined to me and heard my cry.

PRAISE

Yours, Lord, is the greatness, the power,
the glory, the splendour and the majesty;
for everything in heaven and on earth is yours.
All things come from you,
and of your own do we give you.

Prayer at the Preparation of the Table, Common Worship

READING Luke 2.41-43,45-49

Now it was the practice of his parents to go to Jerusalem
every year for the Passover festival; and when he was
twelve, they made the pilgrimage as usual. When the
festive season was over and they set off for home, the
boy Jesus stayed behind in Jerusalem . . . When they
could not find him they returned to Jerusalem to look for
him; and after three days they found him sitting in the
temple surrounded by the teachers, listening to them and
putting questions; and all who heard him were amazed at
his intelligence and the answers he gave. His parents

were astonished to see him there, and his mother said to him, 'My son, why have you treated us like this? Your father and I have been anxiously searching for you. 'Why did you search for me?' he said. 'Did you not know that I was bound to be in my Father's house?' But they did not understand what he meant.

REFLECTION

This is the only story in the New Testament that refers to Jesus' own childhood. It is full of hints about his future: for instance, that reference to 'three days' may be a foretaste of the Resurrection. It also introduces us to the sense of mystery that sometimes surrounded Jesus in his adult years. What is it about Jesus of Nazareth that attracts you and yet also leaves you wondering about him?

PRAYER

Pray for any people you may meet this day whom you find puzzling; ask God to give you insight and grace in your dealings with them. Pray for those people who live in constant fear and anxiety because someone they love has gone missing.

Our Father . . .

CONCLUSION

Father, in the day that lies ahead, may I discover more about you and learn the patience that precedes all wisdom, for Jesus' sake. Amen.

WEDNESDAY EVENING

PRESENCE AND PEACE Psalm 4.8

In peace I will lie down and sleep,
for it is you Lord, only, who make me dwell in safety.

The chances are that this day, like many others, has not
been without its stresses. Place all that has happened
into God's hands, and allow his peace to bring you rest.

READING Exodus 6.10-13

Then the Lord said to Moses, 'Go and bid Pharaoh king
of Egypt let the Israelites leave his country.' Moses
protested to the Lord, 'If the Israelites do not listen to
me, how will Pharaoh listen to such a halting speaker as
me?' The Lord then spoke to both Moses and Aaron and
gave them their commission concerning the Israelites and
Pharaoh, which was that they should bring the Israelites
out of Egypt.

REFLECTION

*The ways in which God reveals himself are many and various.
In Moses' case he too was puzzled by God's call upon his life
and felt inadequate for the task. Joseph and Mary were
puzzled by the boy Jesus, and probably only realized the full*

*implications of what had happened many years afterwards.
For all of us who try to know God and to do his will, what we
feel we ought to do is often not at all clear. We need to
remember that God calls us gently, and at his own pace. There
may be times when the call is very clear and others when
everything seems opaque and confused. We need to be patient
and to trust that, if God wants us to do something, he will
show us what that is in his own good time.*

CONFESSION

Lord God, I offer you myself as I truly am; please forgive
what needs to be forgiven, and grant me, I pray, the courage
to live my life with integrity and truth, for Jesus' sake. Amen.

PRAYER

Keep watch, O Lord, over those who watch, or wake, or
weep tonight, and give your angels charge over those
who sleep. Tend your sick ones, O Lord Christ; rest your
weary ones; bless your dying ones; soothe your suffering
ones; pity your afflicted ones; shield your joyous ones,
and all for your love's sake. Amen.

St Augustine (354–430)

Our Father . . .

CONCLUSION

Lord of the day and the night, I commit myself, and all
whom I love, into your most loving arms, now and for
evermore. Amen.

THURSDAY MORNING

PRESENCE AND PEACE Psalm 57.8
My heart is ready, O God, my heart is ready,
I will sing and give you praise.

PRAISE
Were the whole realm of nature mine,
that were an offering far too small.
Love so amazing, so divine,
demands my soul, my life, my all.
Isaac Watts 1674–1748

READING Mark 1.4-5, 7-8
John the Baptist appeared in the wilderness proclaiming a
baptism in token of repentance, for the forgiveness of
sins; and everyone flocked out to him from the
countryside of Judaea and the city of Jerusalem, and they
were baptized by him in the river Jordan, confessing their
sins . . . He proclaimed: 'After me comes one mightier
than I am, whose sandals I am not worthy to stoop down
and unfasten. I have baptized you with water; he will
baptize you with the Holy Spirit.'

REFLECTION

There is something total and uncompromising about John the Baptist, a figure of power and zeal. Yet he pointed the crowds away from himself, and towards Jesus.

The people who had flocked out to the Judaean wilderness must have been tingling with expectation. Something was about to happen. But no one, not even John, quite knew what it would be. In the event, the arrival of Jesus would change the entire world. If the present and the future are charged with the presence of the risen Christ, what should we do to prepare to be met by him?

PRAYER

Give thanks to God for the unknowns that lie ahead this day, and ask God to help you to discern his presence in whatever may happen. Pray for all those people who live in fear of the future. Pray for all those whose lives may be in danger this day.

Our Father . . .

CONCLUSION

Here, Lord, is my life.
I place it on the altar today.
Use it as you will.
Albert Schweitzer (1875–1965)

THURSDAY EVENING

PRESENCE AND PEACE Psalm 100.4

For the Lord is gracious;
    his steadfast love is everlasting,
and his faithfulness endures
    from generation to generation.

READING Isaiah 62.10-12

Pass through the gates, go out, clear a road for my
people; build a highway, build it up, remove the boulders;
hoist a signal for the peoples.
This is the Lord's proclamation to earth's farthest
bounds: Tell the daughter of Zion, 'See, your deliverance
comes. His reward is with him, his recompense before
him.' They will be called the Holy People, the Redeemed
of the Lord; and you will be called Sought After, City No
Longer Forsaken.

REFLECTION

*Throughout the Old Testament, and repeated in the story of
John the Baptist, is the theme of God coming to gather his
people to himself. The people may have strayed a long way
from what God has asked of them, but he promises
redemption and deliverance. He promises to restore the broken*

*relationship and to take his people to their heavenly city, the
New Jerusalem. There are times in our own lives when we
suffer from broken relationships, with people and with God.
At those times, our sense of wretchedness is dreadful. Our lives
seem worthless and we lose hope. Yet even at our lowest point
we can cling on to the truth, that God will restore us and will
lead us into a new and redeemed land.*

CONFESSION

Lord, your love and mercy are beyond all telling;
look upon me, your servant, with a compassionate heart,
and restore my life to wholeness of body, mind and soul
for the sake of your Son, Jesus Christ my Lord. Amen.

PRAYER

*Pray for those who are desperate for forgiveness, but do not
know how, or where, to find it.
Pray for those you find it difficult to forgive.*

Our Father . . .

CONCLUSION

Lord of all power and might,
I offer myself, and all whom I love, to you this night.
Let your holy angels surround us
with the peace and joy of heaven,
for Jesus' sake. Amen.

FRIDAY MORNING

PRESENCE AND PEACE Psalm 104.2
You are clothed with majesty and honour,
wrapped in light as in a garment.

PRAISE Psalm 106.49
Blessed be the Lord, the God of Israel,
    from everlasting and to everlasting;
and let all the people say, Amen.
    Alleluia.

READING Mark 1.9-11
It was at this time that Jesus came from Nazareth in
Galilee and was baptized in the Jordan by John. As he
was coming up out of the water, he saw the heavens
break open and the Spirit descend on him, like a dove.
And a voice came from heaven: 'You are my beloved Son;
in you I take delight.'

REFLECTION
*In these few words we have just read, Mark condenses an
entire theological world. The Spirit descends upon Jesus. A
voice echoes out of heaven and announces who Jesus really is.
It's all a bit puzzling for us, in our generation, who rightly*

want to ask lots of questions about the story. Did a voice really call out? If so, did others hear it? Why is the Spirit described as being like a dove? We do know that in the book of Genesis the spirit of God is also described like a bird hovering over the waters. This is Mark, announcing in highly pictorial and poetic language, who Jesus is. He is the beginning of a new creation . . .

PRAYER
Pray that this day you may be aware of the vast depths of eternity and be able to see the things of this world in that light. Give thanks to God for your own baptism. Pray for all the people who were with you when you were baptized, and pray for the church in which your baptism took place.

Our Father . . .

CONCLUSION
O gracious and holy Father,
    give us wisdom to perceive you,
intelligence to understand you,
diligence to seek you,
patience to wait for you,
eyes to behold you,
a heart to meditate upon you,
and a life to proclaim you,
through the power of the Spirit of Jesus Christ our lord.
Attributed to St Benedict (480–543)

PRESENCE AND PEACE Psalm 104.1,3

Bless the Lord, O my soul,
O Lord my God how excellent is your greatness! . . .
You spread out the heavens like a curtain
and lay the beams of your dwelling place in the waters
above.

READING Genesis 1.1-5

In the beginning God created the heavens and the earth.
The earth was a vast waste, darkness covered the deep,
and the spirit of God hovered over the surface of the
water. God said, 'Let there be light', and there was light;
and God saw the light was good, and he separated light
from darkness. He called the light day, and the darkness
night. So evening came, and morning came; it was the
first day.

REFLECTION

There has been much discussion, from the nineteenth century
onwards, about the story of creation in the book of Genesis
and about whether it can stand up to scientific scrutiny.
That's to miss the point. Genesis is a way of saying that the
universe and the earth have purpose. The story is about why

things are, not about how things are. The image of God
hovering above the waters of chaos, and bringing shape and
direction to life, is an enchanting one. If you think of the word
'Spirit' meaning 'energy', you will be close to that sense of
wonder that pervades this ancient and beautiful story.
Imagine the infinite reaches of space soaring above you; is it
not breathtaking to think that all of it has been brought into
being by love?

CONFESSION

Lord of the universe, forgive my doubt, and open my
mind to the possibility of your eternal love, constantly at
work in my life and the life of all that is.

PRAYER

Bring to mind something in the natural world that has caught
your eye today, and give thanks to God for it. Pray for all
involved in astronomy and space research. Pray that you may
use your own gifts of reasoning with humility and grace.

Our Father . . .

CONCLUSION

Most loving Creator and Redeemer, you hold all things in
being. I give you thanks and praise, simply that you are;
and, for the rest, please accept my knowing and my
unknowing, as a prayer from my wondering heart.

WEEK THREE

MONDAY MORNING

PRESENCE AND PEACE Psalm 105.4

Seek the Lord and his strength;
seek his face continually.

At the beginning of a new day, O Lord, let your strength
guide and uphold me. Grant me wisdom, grant me
courage, but, above all, grant me a loving heart, through
Jesus Christ our Lord.

PRAISE

Praise to the holiest in the height,
and in the depths be praise,
in all his words most wonderful,
most sure in all his ways.

John Henry Newman (1801–90)

READING Mark 1.12-13

At once the Spirit drove him out into the wilderness, and
there he remained for forty days tempted by Satan. He
was among the wild beasts; and angels attended to his
needs.

REFLECTION

Following the climactic event of his baptism, Jesus felt compelled to go out into the wilderness. It was a time of trial, an immense ordeal, as he tried to understand what he should do. The intensity of this experience is difficult to imagine. Mark conveys how terrible it was by referring to the representatives of hell and heaven, the Satan and the angels, being with Jesus in the desert; Satan trying to deflect him from his true call, and the angels bringing him succour and strength. Our own times of testing cannot be avoided, but how we deal with them is crucial. There is nothing we can undergo that can separate us from God's unbreakable love.

PRAYER

Pray for all those who may be enduring great tests and trials this day. Pray for yourself that in your own times of testing you may hold fast to Christ.

Our Father . . .

CONCLUSION

Father in heaven,
look with mercy upon us in all we undergo,
and so fill us with the Spirit
that we may be strong and very courageous,
true followers of your Son, our Saviour, Jesus Christ.
Amen.

MONDAY EVENING

PRESENCE AND PEACE Isaiah 46.9-10

I am God, and there is no one like me.
From the beginning I reveal the end,
from ancient times what is yet to be;
I say, 'My purpose stands,
I shall accomplish all that I please.'

READING Exodus 16.2-7

The Israelites all complained to Moses and Aaron in the wilderness. They said, 'If only we had died at the Lord's hand in Egypt, where we sat by the fleshpots and had plenty of bread! But you have brought us out into this wilderness to let this whole assembly starve to death.' The Lord said to Moses, 'I shall rain down bread from heaven for you. Each day the people are to go out and gather a day's supply, so that I can put them to the test and see whether they follow my instructions or not. But on the sixth day, when they prepare what they bring in, it should be twice as much as they gather on other days.' Moses and Aaron said to all the Israelites, 'In the evening you will know that it was the Lord who brought you out of Egypt, and in the morning you will see the glory of the Lord, because he has listened to your complaints against him.'

REFLECTION

It was through the wilderness that Moses led the people until they reached the Promised Land. It was into the wilderness that Jesus felt compelled to go at the beginning of his ministry. Being in a desert place away from the distractions of the world has been a theme that has continued in Christianity. While, for many of us, spending time in a desert is not an option, we all know what it is to be in desolation. God took his people through their wilderness years, and we can be sure that he will be present with us whenever we find ourselves in the wildernesses of our own experience.

CONFESSION

Lord God, wipe away the sin from my eyes, and restore my sight, that I may see you in your love and in your glory, for Jesus Christ, his sake.

PRAYER

Pray for all those people you know who are stricken by grief. Pray for any situation you may be in that leaves you feeling deeply troubled.

Our Father . . .

CONCLUSION

God of the future, lead me with bonds of love towards the purpose you have for me, and for the world, in Jesus Christ my Lord. Amen.

TUESDAY MORNING

PRESENCE AND PEACE Psalm 9.1-2
I will give thanks to you, Lord, with my whole heart;
I will tell of all your marvellous works.
I will be glad and rejoice in you;
I will make music to your name, O Most High.

Let the song of your love, and the music of your glory, be
always on my lips and in my heart, O Lord my Saviour,
and my most merciful Redeemer. Amen.

PRAISE Psalm 103.1
Bless the Lord, O my soul,
and all that is within me bless his holy name.

READING Mark 1.14-15
After John had been arrested, Jesus came into Galilee
proclaiming the gospel of God: 'The time has arrived; the
kingdom of God is upon you. Repent, and believe the
gospel.'

REFLECTION
*Mark wastes no time in the telling of the story of Jesus. One
minute Jesus is wrestling with the powers of darkness in the*

*wilderness, the next he is striding through Galilee proclaiming
his message. It is as though the urgency of Jesus' message has
been translated directly by Mark onto the page.*

*But Mark is also condensing the story. Here, in these two
verses, he sets out the key point of Jesus' teaching: it's all
about the kingdom of God breaking out of eternity and into
time. And what Mark goes on to suggest is that, if we want to
know what the kingdom is like, we shall see it in Jesus.*

What is it about Jesus that claims your attention?

PRAYER

*Give thanks for the day that lies ahead, and ask that you may
have the grace and wisdom to discern the kingdom of God at
work in the world.*

*Pray for all those people you will be working with this day and
for all who work in your sector of the economy.*

Pray for all those people who face this day with no hope.

Our Father . . .

CONCLUSION

God of power and might, you come to us with such
humility that we often fail to see you in our midst; grant
us this day, a vision of our world radiant with your glory;
through Jesus Christ our Lord. Amen.

TUESDAY EVENING

PRESENCE AND PEACE Isaiah 45.22

From every corner of the earth
turn to me and be saved;
for I am God, there is none other.

READING Isaiah 52.7-9

How beautiful on the mountains
    are the feet of the herald,
the bringer of good news, announcing deliverance,
proclaiming to Zion, 'Your God has become king.'
Your watchmen raise their voices
    and shout together in joy;
for with their own eyes they see the Lord return to Zion.
Break forth together into shouts of joy,
    you ruins of Jerusalem;
for the Lord has comforted his people,
    he has redeemed Jerusalem.

REFLECTION

*The words of Isaiah ring out with joy. There is a palpable
sense of redemption being offered, and things that were
broken being made new. That sense of hope in God has
sustained the people of Israel from time immemorial, and has*

*become part of the faith of followers of Jesus. Do you feel that
there is a place in your life for that same sense of hope?*

CONFESSION

Most merciful God,
we confess to you,
before the whole company of heaven and one another,
that we have sinned in thought, word and deed
and in what we have failed to do.
Forgive us our sins,
heal us by your Spirit
and raise us to new life in Christ. Amen.

Compline, Common Worship

PRAYER

*Pray for your local church and its leaders.
Give thanks for the gift of forgiveness.*

Our Father . . .

CONCLUSION

Lord God, I turn to you this night simply as I am, with all
my weakness, with my doubts and failures; come to me, I
pray, and grant me inward peace, so that, when the
morning comes, I may be refreshed and ready for your
service, through Jesus Christ our Lord. Amen.

WEDNESDAY MORNING

PRESENCE AND PEACE Psalm 6.4
Turn again, O Lord, and deliver my soul;
save me for your loving mercy's sake.

Lord God,
you steal into my soul like the beauty of the dawn;
may my life this day be filled with your light and peace,
for Jesus' sake. Amen.

PRAISE Psalm 103.20
Bless the Lord, you angels of his,
you mighty ones who do his bidding
    and hearken to the voice of his word.

READING Mark 1.16-20
Jesus was walking by the sea of Galilee when he saw
Simon and his brother Andrew at work with casting nets
in the lake; for they were fishermen. Jesus said to them,
'Come, follow me, and I will make you fishers of men.' At
once they left their nets and followed him.
Going a little farther, he saw James son of Zebedee and
his brother John in a boat mending their nets. At once he

called them; and they left their father Zebedee in the boat with the hired men and followed him.

REFLECTION

There is something about Jesus that makes us radically reassess our lives. In the case of the first disciples they gave up their livelihood and followed him. For us the call may be equally demanding, though for others it will be a call to stay where they are and serve God there.
What do you think Jesus is calling you to do?

PRAYER

Give thanks for all those people who have followed Christ where he has led. Give thanks for the first disciples, for their courage and their willingness to go into an unknown future.

Lord God, in the stillness of the morning, make your ways known to us and give us the strength to follow you, wherever you may lead, for Jesus' sake. Amen.

Our Father . . .

CONCLUSION

O Lord Jesus Christ, who created and redeemed me, and brought me to that which now I am, you know what you would do with me; do with me according to your will; for your tender mercy's sake.
King Henry VI (1421–72)

WEDNESDAY EVENING

PRESENCE AND PEACE Romans 8.16-17

The Spirit of God affirms to our spirit that we are God's children; and if children, then heirs, heirs of God and fellow-heirs with Christ; but we must share his sufferings if we are also to share his glory.

READING Isaiah 42.1-4

Here is my servant, whom I uphold,
my chosen one, in whom I take delight!
I have put my spirit in him;
he will establish justice among the nations.
He will not shout or raise his voice,
or make himself heard in the street.
He will not break a crushed reed
or snuff out a smouldering wick;
unfailingly he will establish justice.
He will never falter or be crushed
until he sets justice on earth,
while coasts and islands await his teaching.

REFLECTION

Isaiah writes poetry of great beauty. He tells the people of Israel that God's servant, in whom he takes great delight, will bring justice to the earth. God, says Isaiah, has poured the Spirit upon his chosen one, in order to equip him for the task that lies ahead. It has been the experience of Christians across the centuries that God continues to pour his energy and strength upon them. As we learn to follow Christ as his disciples, God, in his grace, will be with us in all we do. It is an enormous comfort.

CONFESSION

Lord God, when my courage fails me,
or when I am in despair,
please look upon me with mercy,
and raise me up to follow you anew, for Jesus' sake.

PRAYER

Give thanks for all who have gone out across the world with the gospel of Christ.
Pray for all those people who are treated unjustly.
Pray for all those who administer the law in our own country.

Our Father . . .

CONCLUSION

May the right hand of God keep us ever in old age, the grace of Christ keep us from the enemy. O Lord, direct our heart in the way of peace; through Jesus Christ our Lord.
Bishop Aedelwald (eighth century)

THURSDAY MORNING

PRESENCE AND PRAISE Isaiah 60.1
Arise, shine, Jerusalem, for your light has come;
and over you the glory of the Lord has dawned.

Almighty and everlasting God, your power is revealed in
weakness, your love in humility and grace; make my soul
your dwelling place that I may walk in the way of Christ,
this day and always. Amen.

PRAISE Judith 16.13
I will sing a new hymn to my God:
O Lord, you are great and glorious,
you are marvellous in your strength, invincible.

READING Mark 1.21-28
They came to Capernaum, and on the sabbath he went
to the synagogue and began to teach. The people were
amazed at his teaching, for, unlike the scribes, he taught
with a note of authority. Now there was a man in their
synagogue possessed by an unclean spirit. He shrieked at
him: 'What do you want with us, Jesus of Nazareth? Have
you come to destroy us? I know who you are – the Holy
One of God.' Jesus rebuked him: 'Be silent', he said, 'and

come out of him.' The unclean spirit threw the man into convulsions and with a loud cry left him. They were all amazed and began to ask one another, 'What is this? A new kind of teaching! He speaks with authority. When he gives orders, even the unclean spirits obey.' His fame soon spread far and wide throughout Galilee.

REFLECTION

Mark's first chapter is a kind of overture to the whole Gospel. In it are to be found many of the themes that will emerge in the rest of the work, including miracles of healing. Such miracles raise a number of questions for us in the twenty-first century, but what we cannot avoid are the questions that were asked by those first witnesses. Who is Jesus? What is the source of his authority?

PRAYER

Pray that in the day that lies ahead you may exercise with integrity any authority you have. Pray for all who exercise authority over others, that they may be just and fair in all their dealings. Pray for all who feel bullied and harassed at work.

Our Father . . .

CONCLUSION

Lord Jesus Christ, from whom all peace and healing flow, bring your most loving peace and healing to my soul. Amen.

THURSDAY EVENING

PRESENCE AND PEACE Psalm 73.26

Though my flesh and my heart fail me,
God is the strength of my heart and my portion for ever.

Father, may I rest in your strength and trust in your love,
now and always. Amen.

PRAISE Psalm 71.19

Your righteousness, O God, reaches to the heavens;
in the great things you have done, who is like you,
O God?

READING Jeremiah 1.4-10

This word of the Lord came to me: 'Before I formed you
in the womb I chose you, and before you were born I
consecrated you; I appointed you a prophet to the
nations.' 'Ah! Lord God,' I answered, 'I am not skilled in
speaking; I am too young.' But the Lord said, 'Do not
plead that you are too young; for you are to go to
whatever people I send you, and say whatever I tell you
to say.

REFLECTION

Jeremiah was not convinced that he had the gifts required of a prophet, but he was assured by God that he would receive the strength and wisdom he needed for the task to which he had been called. When any of us feel inadequate to answer God's call we are in good company, yet God does provide, and it is God's grace that supports us.

CONFESSION

Lord God, look upon me with mercy, sinner that I am, and encourage my soul with your unending love, through Jesus Christ our Lord.

PRAYER

Give thanks for all those moments in the day in which you have been assured of God's enduring presence.
Pray for all those who abuse authority and for those who suffer as a result.

Our Father . . .

CONCLUSION

Lord God,
you reveal your power in weakness,
grant me the grace to trust your wisdom,
now and always.

FRIDAY MORNING

PRESENCE AND PRAISE Psalm 85.10

Mercy and truth are met together,
righteousness and peace have kissed each other.

Lord Jesus Christ, when I pray, please accept my words,
my silence, my confusion, and my questions as my prayer,
and then guide me so that my prayer may become more
like yours . . .

PRAISE

We praise you, O God,
we acclaim you as the Lord;
all creation worships you,
the Father everlasting.

Te Deum Laudamus, Common Worship

READING Mark 1.32-37

That evening after sunset they brought to him all who
were ill or possessed by demons; and the whole town
was there, gathered at the door. He healed many who
suffered from various diseases, and drove out many
demons. He would not let the demons speak, because
they knew who he was.

Very early next morning he got up and went out. He went away to a remote spot and remained there in prayer. But Simon and his companions went in search of him, and when they found him, they said, 'Everybody is looking for you.'

REFLECTION

To pray, no matter what or how we pray, is to follow in the footsteps of Jesus. He was in need of peace after a tumultuous day and he needed time to be with God. That is what prayer is, time spent with God; sometimes using words, and sometimes just being in silence with him.

PRAYER

Give thanks for moments of silence, snatched out of the maelstrom of a working day.
Pray for all those working in highly pressurized environments, particularly in financial trading and banking.

Our Father . . .

CONCLUSION

Lord of beauty,
you make yourself known in the silence of my heart;
grant me the patience to learn deep stillness,
that I may be drawn closer to you, for Jesus' sake. Amen.

FRIDAY EVENING

PRESENCE AND PEACE Psalm 145.19
The Lord is near to those who call upon him,
to all who call upon him faithfully.

Lord, the music of your love sings through all creation;
still my soul that I may hear you, and be renewed by your
eternal beauty.

PRAISE Revelation 4.11
You are worthy, O Lord our God, to receive glory and
honour and power, because you created all things; by
your will they were created and have their being!

READING Isaiah 65.1-2
I was ready to respond, but no one asked,
ready to be found, but no one sought me.
I said, 'Here am I! Here am I!'
to a nation that did not invoke me by name.
All day long I held out my hands
appealing to a rebellious people
who went their evil way,
in pursuit of their own devices.

REFLECTION

Time and time again the prophets in the Old Testament call the people back to God; to God who longs for them to approach him. God yearns, with all his heart, for his people to be reconciled to him. In prayer we are expressing our human yearning for God, and we are met by God's yearning for us. In Christ we are offered a way in which those inexpressible longings between heaven and earth can be brought to a glorious fruition. When God calls out, 'Here am I', what is our response?

CONFESSION

When you call and I do not listen, have mercy upon me; have mercy upon me, most loving Lord, for Jesus' sake.

PRAYER

Give thanks to God for his infinite patience.
Give thanks for another working week completed and for the weekend that lies ahead.

Our Father . . .

CONCLUSION

May God the Father bless us; may Christ take care of us, the Holy Spirit enlighten us all the days of our life. The Lord be our defender and keeper now and for ever.

Prayer of St Hedelward

WEEK FOUR

MONDAY MORNING

PRESENCE AND PRAISE Psalm 65.9

The river of God is full of water;
you prepare grain for your people,
    for so you provide for the earth.

O God and heavenly King,
you pour your love and goodness upon the earth:
give us thankful hearts,
that we may reflect your glory in our lives,
through Jesus Christ our Lord. Amen.

PRAISE Psalm 68.18

Blessed be the Lord who bears our burdens day by day,
for God is our salvation.

READING Mark 4.30-32

He said, 'How shall we picture the kingdom of God, or
what parable shall we use to describe it? It is like a
mustard seed; when sown in the ground it is smaller than
any other seed, but once sown, it springs up and grows
taller than any other plant, and forms branches so large
that birds can roost in its shade.'

REFLECTION

One of Jesus' key messages was about the kingdom of God. It is an elusive concept, sometimes appearing as though it is already amongst us, and at other times seeming to be a long way off in the future.
The Early Church believed that the kingdom was realized in the life, death, resurrection and ascension of Jesus; and, as Jesus has entered eternity where time is no more, so the kingdom is present at every moment, through the prodigal, outpouring generosity of the Holy Spirit.

PRAYER

Pray for the day that lies ahead, that in it you may glimpse the work of God.
Pray for those who work in agriculture and the food industry.

Our Father . . .

CONCLUSION

Eternal God and Father, by whose power we are created and by whose love we are redeemed: guide and strengthen us by your Spirit that we may give ourselves to your service and live this day in love to one another and to you, through Jesus Christ our Lord.
Joint Liturgical Group

MONDAY EVENING

PRESENCE AND PEACE Psalm 31.24
Be strong and let your heart take courage,
all you who wait in hope for the Lord.

Lord God and heavenly Father, you are the source of
beauty, grace and truth; fill my soul with your most holy
love that I may sing your praise all my days, through Jesus
Christ our Lord. Amen.

PRAISE Psalm 30.4
Sing to the Lord, you servants of his;
give thanks to his holy name.

READING Mark 9.33-37
So they came to Capernaum; and when he had gone
indoors, he asked them, 'What were you arguing about
on the way?' They were silent, because on the way they
had been discussing which of them was the greatest. So
he sat down, called the Twelve, and said to them, 'If
anyone wants to be first, he must make himself last of all
and servant of all.' Then he took a child, set him in front
of them, and put his arm around him. 'Whoever receives
a child like this in my name,' he said, 'receives me; and

whoever receives me, receives not me but the One who sent me.'

REFLECTION

There are times when the humanity of Jesus' disciples breaks out from the text. This is one such moment. The disciples are squabbling like adolescents, about which of them is the greatest. Jesus' response is to remind them of the importance of being like a servant, and he demonstrates that it is in receiving things with humility, like a child, that God is to be found. Is servanthood a characteristic of your life?

CONFESSION

Lord, I confess to you my arrogance and pride; restore in me, I pray, a proper judgement of who I am, and grant me a new and humble heart, for Jesus' sake. Amen.

PRAYER

Give thanks for those who serve the country in the Civil Service and in local and national government. Pray for those whom you are called to love and serve in Christ's name.

Our Father . . .

CONCLUSION

May the Lord bless us,
may he keep us from all evil,
and lead us to life everlasting. Amen.

TUESDAY MORNING

PRESENCE AND PEACE Psalm 138.8
The Lord shall make good his purpose for me;
your loving-kindness, O Lord endures for ever;
    forsake not the work of your hands.

Lord Jesus Christ, you are the way to the Father; teach
me to walk in your way, all the days of my life, for your
mercy and for your truth's sake. Amen.

PRAISE Psalm 145.3
Great is the Lord and highly to be praised;
his greatness is beyond all searching out.

READING Mark 10.32
They were on the road going up to Jerusalem, and Jesus
was leading the way; and the disciples were filled with
awe, while those who followed behind were afraid.
Once again he took the Twelve aside and began to tell
them what was to happen to him.

REFLECTION

One of the temptations for followers of Jesus is to try to tame him, to make him seem much simpler than he was.
In this account from Mark we are given a glimpse of that otherness of Jesus that left even his closest friends in a state of bewilderment verging on fear. As Jesus led the way up to Jerusalem the disciples were in awe of him.
Is your image of Jesus too cosy? What is it about Jesus that leaves you feeling in awe of him?

PRAYER

Pray for those who have been damaged by a bad experience of Christ's followers.
Pray for all those who face this day in fear.

Our Father . . .

CONCLUSION

Eternal God,
the light of the minds that know you,
the joy of the hearts that love you,
the strength of the wills that serve you;
grant us so to know you that we may truly love you,
so to love you that we may fully serve you,
whose service is perfect freedom,
through Jesus Christ our Lord.
Gelasian Sacramentary (seventh century)

PRESENCE AND PEACE
Lord God, King of the universe, let your love and peace keep me in safety this night, through Jesus Christ our Lord.

PRAISE Psalm 86.12
I will thank you, O Lord my God, with all my heart, and glorify your name for evermore.

READING Mark 12.28-31
Then one of the scribes, who had been listening to these discussions and had observed how well Jesus answered, came forward and asked him, 'Which is the first of all the commandments?' He answered, 'The first is, "Hear O Israel: the Lord our God is the one Lord, and you must love the Lord your God with all your heart, with all your soul, with all your mind, and with all your strength." The second is this: "You must love your neighbour as yourself." No other commandment is greater than these.'

REFLECTION
How should we live? In the story in Mark's Gospel about an encounter between a scribe and Jesus, the answer to the

question is given. It is all about loving God, and loving our neighbour.

CONFESSION

Most merciful God,
Father of our Lord Jesus Christ,
we confess that we have sinned
in thought, word and deed.
We have not loved you with our whole heart.
We have not loved our neighbours as ourselves.
In your mercy
forgive what we have been,
help us to amend what we are,
and direct what we shall be;
that we may do justly, love mercy,
and walk humbly with you, our God.
Prayers of Penitence, Common Worship

PRAYER

Give thanks for all those people who have shown you grace and love this day. Pray for the peace of the world.

Our Father . . .

CONCLUSION

Loving heavenly Father, I place into your hands my self, my soul and my body; grant me your peace, now and always.

WEDNESDAY MORNING

PRESENCE AND PRAISE Psalm 62.5
Wait on God alone in stillness, O my soul;
for in him is my hope.

Lord God,
You are the source of all stillness and peace;
let my heart rest in you, and you alone,
this day and for evermore.

PRAISE Psalm 66.1
Be joyful in God, all the earth;
sing the glory of his name;
 sing the glory of his praise.

READING Mark 14.3-6,8-9
Jesus was at Bethany, in the house of Simon the leper. As
he sat at table, a woman came in carrying a bottle of very
costly perfume, pure oil of nard. She broke it open and
poured the oil over his head. Some of those present said
indignantly to one another, 'Why this waste? The
perfume might have been sold for more than three
hundred denarii and the money given to the poor'; and
they began to scold her. But Jesus said, 'Leave her alone.

Why make trouble for her? It is a fine thing she has done for me . . . She has done what lay in her power; she has anointed my body in anticipation of my burial. Truly I tell you: wherever the gospel is proclaimed throughout the world, what she has done will be told as her memorial.'

REFLECTION

Such a prodigal and generous act of spontaneous beauty releases in the bystanders a spiteful bout of self-righteous moralizing. Jesus accepts the gift and promises that the woman's action will be for ever associated with him and will therefore have a place in the Gospel. He redeems and blesses her generous action. Self-righteousness is a destructive trait, because it hardens our hearts to compassion and prevents generosity. What will you do this day to increase the spirit of generosity in society?

PRAYER

Give thanks for people whose generosity of spirit has changed the world. Pray that you may increase in generosity of heart and soul and mind.

Our Father . . .

CONCLUSION

Father in heaven, give me the strength, I pray, to be generous in thought, generous in word and generous in deed, this day and always, through Jesus Christ our Lord.

WEDNESDAY EVENING

PRESENCE AND PEACE Psalm 42.1
As the deer longs for the water brooks,
so longs my soul for you, O God.

Lord, you refresh my soul with the water of life;
I bless you for the gift of your love,
outpoured upon me,
and upon the world,
through Jesus Christ our Saviour.

PRAISE Psalm 42.14
O put your trust in God;
for I will yet give him thanks,
    who is the help of my countenance, and my God.

READING Mark 14.17,22-26
In the evening he came to the house with the Twelve . . .
During supper he took bread, and having said the
blessing he broke it and gave it to them, with the words:
'Take this; this is my body.' Then he took a cup, and
having offered thanks to God he gave it to them; and
they all drank from it. And he said to them, 'This is my
blood, the blood of the covenant, shed for many. Truly I

tell you: never again shall I drink from the fruit of the vine until that day when I drink it new in the kingdom of God.'

REFLECTION

Jesus had prepared the last meal he would have with his disciples with great forethought. The room was booked, the food was ready, and the disciples gathered in the Upper Room with a sense of heightened excitement and, perhaps, apprehension. And then Jesus said words, and enacted a drama, that have been at the heart of the Church ever since. In the bread and wine, Christians have known, and continue to know, the very presence of Christ. Are you open to receive the life of Christ himself?

PRAYER

Give thanks for all those meals you have had with family or friends, which have been filled with affection and joy. Pray for any people you know who are hungry for the love of God. Place yourself, and all whom you love, into the refreshing beauty of God this night.

Our Father . . .

CONCLUSION

Lord God, create in me, I pray, a heart filled with thanksgiving.

THURSDAY MORNING

PRESENCE AND PEACE

Lord God,
you are my stronghold,
you are my might,
you are my fortress and defence;
let me shelter in your unending strength,
now and always, for Jesus' sake. Amen.

PRAISE Psalm 31.7

I will be glad and rejoice in your mercy,
for you have seen my affliction
   and known my soul in adversity.

READING Mark 14.32-36

When they reached a place called Gethsemane, he said to
his disciples, 'Sit here while I pray.' And he took Peter and
James and John with him. Horror and anguish overwhelmed
him, and he said to them, 'My heart is ready to break with
grief; stop here, and stay awake.' Then he went on a little
farther, threw himself on the ground, and prayed that if it
were possible this hour might pass him by. 'Abba, Father,' he
said, 'all things are possible to you; take this cup from me.
Yet not my will but yours.'

REFLECTION

As we follow Jesus during his last days on earth the events come thick and fast. We may be spared some of the details by Mark, but he gives us more than enough to help us enter into those last days in our imaginations. The anguish of Christ is terrible; a sense of impending death hangs over everything. It is no wonder that Christ throws himself on the ground in prayer. All we can do is to watch and wait.

What are the challenges that God is making on your life that you find really hard?

PRAYER

Pray that in your following of Christ you may know his strength and help in times of direst need. Pray for yourself and all those who feel that they have failed Christ.

Our Father . . .

CONCLUSION

O most loving Father,
grant us the grace to do your will,
the strength to walk in your way,
and the courage to fulfil your purposes
of love for our world,
through Jesus Christ our Lord. Amen.

THURSDAY EVENING

PRESENCE AND PEACE

Lord God, at this evening hour I place myself and all
whom I love into your compassionate and healing hands,
through Jesus Christ our Lord, who died and rose again,
and now reigns with you in glory, for ever and ever.
Amen.

PRAISE Psalm 68.19

God is for us the God of our salvation;
God is the Lord who can deliver from death.

READING Mark 15.20,22-27

They brought Jesus to the place called Golgotha, which
means 'Place of a Skull', and they offered him drugged
wine, but he did not take it. Then they fastened him to
the cross. They shared out his clothes, casting lots to
decide what each should have.

It was nine in the morning when they crucified him; and
the inscription giving the charge against him read, 'The
King of the Jews'. Two robbers were crucified with him,
one on his right and the other on his left.

REFLECTION

Mark tells the story of Jesus' last hours with dignity and understatement. He does not wallow in the tortures and horror of it all, but grips our imagination and our hearts by the simplicity of his language. Picture yourself at the scene. With which person in the account that Mark gives do you most identify? Why is this? What does it tell you about yourself? What does it tell you about God?

CONFESSION

Most merciful and loving God, I bring to you my broken and contrite heart for all the sins that I have committed. I repent and turn to you again praying that you will forgive me, through the merits and mediation of Jesus Christ our Lord.

PRAYER

Give thanks for the Passion of Jesus Christ who gave himself for us on the cross. Pray for those who work for reconciliation between races and religions.

Our Father . . .

CONCLUSION

Lord Jesus Christ, you walked the way of the cross that we might know your love; we give you heartfelt thanks for your eternal and most holy sacrifice.

FRIDAY MORNING

PRESENCE AND PEACE

O most holy, O most mighty, O most compassionate and loving God, let me gaze upon you that I may know you; and love you with all my heart, with all my soul, with all my mind, and with all my strength, now and for evermore. Amen.

PRAISE Psalm 77.13

Your way, O God, is holy;
who is so great a god as our God?

READING Mark 15.33-39

At midday a darkness fell over the whole land, which lasted till three in the afternoon; and at three Jesus cried aloud . . . 'My God, my God, why have you forsaken me?' Hearing this, some of the bystanders said, 'Listen! He is calling Elijah.' Someone ran and soaked a sponge in sour wine and held it to his lips on the end of a stick. 'Let us see', he said, 'If Elijah will come to take him down.' Then Jesus gave a loud cry and died; and the curtain of the temple was torn in two from top to bottom. When the centurion who was standing opposite him saw how he died, he said, 'This man must have been a son of God.'

REFLECTION

The anguish of Christ's sense of dereliction is unbearable. Even in death he was misunderstood, and even in death it required an unbeliever to state who Christ was. The old order had changed (the veil of the Temple was torn in two) and we await what is to be revealed. But, for the moment, we can only gaze on the scene and ask God to have mercy upon us.

PRAYER

Ask God to help you to understand the meaning of Christ's death in your mind and in your soul.

Pray for those who are dying and for those who wait with them, and for all those who work in hospices and palliative care.

Pray that this day you may allow the death of Jesus to shape your actions and your thoughts.

Our Father . . .

CONCLUSION

Lord Jesus Christ, you entered the portals of death
    that we might be brought to the gates of heaven;
we bless you, we praise you,
    we kneel at the foot of the cross and adore you,
you alone are our Saviour
    and our most mighty Redeemer.
Amen.

FRIDAY EVENING

PRESENCE AND PEACE

Lord, in the darkness of this night, be present to my soul
that I may be at peace, and rest in your unfailing love,
through Jesus Christ our Lord.

PRAISE Psalm 43.6

O put your trust in God;
for I will yet give him thanks,
    who is the help of my countenance, and my God.

READING Mark 15.42-47

By this time evening had come; and as it was the day of
preparation (that is, the day before the sabbath), Joseph
of Arimathaea, a respected member of the Council, a
man who looked forward to the kingdom of God,
bravely went in to Pilate and asked for the body of Jesus.
Pilate was surprised to hear that he had died so soon, and
sent for the centurion to make sure that he was already
dead. And when he heard the centurion's report, he gave
Joseph leave to take the body. So Joseph bought a linen
sheet, took him down from the cross, and wrapped him
in the sheet. Then he laid him in a tomb cut out of the
rock, and rolled a stone against the entrance. And Mary

of Magdala and Mary the mother of Jesus were watching
and saw where he was laid.

REFLECTION

*There are some people who enter the Gospel story briefly and
you want to know more about them. Joseph of Arimathaea
who takes the body of Jesus from the cross is one of those
people. Yet after this mention in Mark, he disappears from the
record. All we can do is to speculate why he had the courage
and the compassion to look after the corpse of Christ. Would
you have done the same?*

CONFESSION

O Saviour of the world, by your cross and precious blood
you have redeemed us, save us and help us we humbly
beseech you, O Lord.

PRAYER

*Give thanks for all those people who, in a moment of
challenge, have the courage to respond with generosity.
Pray that you may have the grace to keep watch with Christ
throughout your life.*

Our Father . . .

CONCLUSION

Lord God, grant me the grace to serve you and all people
with self-denying love; for Jesus' sake.

week
FIVE

MONDAY MORNING

PRESENCE AND PEACE
Almighty and most faithful God,
your love is unending, your beauty beyond all telling;
may your spirit dwell in my heart, now and for ever,
through Jesus Christ, our risen Lord and Saviour. Amen.

PRAISE Psalm 117.1
O praise the Lord, all you nations;
praise him, all you peoples.

READING Luke 24.13-16
That same day two of them were on their way to a
village called Emmaus, about seven miles from Jerusalem,
talking together about all that had happened. As they
talked and argued, Jesus himself came up and walked
with them; but something prevented them from
recognizing him . . .

REFLECTION
*You may well know the rest of that story told by Luke; how
Jesus explained to the men that the events in Jerusalem had
been foretold by the prophets. Still they did not recognize him.
When they got to the house where they were going, they*

invited the stranger to join them. He went with them and, at table, took bread, gave a blessing, broke the bread and offered it to them; immediately they recognized Jesus, but he vanished from their sight. One of the themes in the stories about the risen Christ in the Gospels is that he was not always recognized, even by his closest friends. But this incomprehension is followed, when he speaks to them, by a moment of awed recognition. Is not this experience one that we share, even if only fleetingly? It is as though we glimpse the risen Christ out of the corner of our eye in certain situations, but then he eludes us.

PRAYER

Give thanks for the Eucharist where bread is taken, blessed, broken and given; where Christ makes himself known to us in great humility. Pray for all who are unable to receive Holy Communion because they live in places where persecution is rife. Pray that in this coming day your eyes may be open to discern the risen Christ.

Our Father . . .

CONCLUSION

Lord Jesus Christ, you make yourself known to us in the breaking of the bread; open our eyes to see you at work in the world, and help us to proclaim you in our words and in our lives. Amen.

MONDAY EVENING

PRESENCE AND PEACE

Lord God, angels and archangels sing your praise in heaven, and on earth all things echo eternity's song; by your grace and mercy may the joy of the risen Christ enter my heart, so that my life may be in harmony and at peace, for his name's sake. Amen.

PRAISE Psalm 16.6

I will bless the Lord who has given me counsel,
and in the night watches he instructs my heart.

READING Matthew 28.16-20

The eleven disciples made their way to Galilee, to the mountain where Jesus had told them to meet him. When they saw him, they knelt in worship, though some were doubtful. Jesus came near and said to them: 'Full authority in heaven and earth has been committed to me. Go therefore to all nations and make them my disciples; baptize them in the name of the Father and the Son and the Holy Spirit, and teach them to observe all that I have commanded you. I will be with you always, to the end of time.'

REFLECTION

In Matthew's account of the days after the Resurrection, the disciples meet Christ on a mountain and there receive their final instructions from him. Even so, there are some of the disciples who cannot believe their eyes or their ears. When we are assailed by doubts we may get comfort from the fact that we are like those first disciples. We need to remember that Jesus' promise about being with them always is made to doubters, as well as to those who seem certain.

CONFESSION

Lord, I believe; help me when belief falls short.

PRAYER

Thank God for the joys you have experienced this day. Pray for those who are actively scornful of belief. Give thanks for family and friends and all those in whose company you sense the joy of heaven.

Our Father . . .

CONCLUSION

Be present, O merciful God, and protect us through the silent hours of this night, so that we who are wearied by the changes and chances of this fleeting world may repose upon your eternal changelessness; through Jesus Christ our Lord.

Common Worship, Night Prayer (Compline)

TUESDAY MORNING

PRESENCE AND PEACE

O God, the creator of all things, let the music of your love enter my soul that I may be at peace, through Jesus Christ, our risen Lord and Saviour. Amen.

PRAISE Psalm 118.1

O give thanks to the Lord, for he is good;
his mercy endures for ever.

READING John 20.11-18

Mary stood outside the tomb weeping. And as she wept, she peered into the tomb, and saw two angels in white sitting there, one at the head, and one at the feet, where the body of Jesus had lain. They asked her, 'Why are you weeping?' She answered, 'They have taken my Lord away, and I do not know where they have laid him.' With these words she turned round and saw Jesus standing there, but she did not recognize him. Jesus asked her, 'Why are you weeping? Who are you looking for?' Thinking it was the gardener, she said, 'If it is you, sir, who removed him, tell me where you have laid him, and I will take him away.' 'Jesus said, 'Mary!' She turned and said to him, 'Rabbuni!' (which is Hebrew for 'Teacher'). 'Do not cling to me,' said Jesus, 'for I have not yet ascended to the Father. But go to my brothers, and tell them that I am ascending to my Father and your Father, to my God and your God.' Mary of Magdala went to tell the disciples. 'I have seen the Lord!' she said, and gave them his message.

REFLECTION

This is one of the most powerful and poignant episodes in the New Testament. The risen Jesus is mistaken for a jobbing gardener. And then comes that dazzling moment of recognition when Jesus speaks Mary's name. When the risen Christ speaks your 'name' to you, that is, when he is so present with you that he knows you totally, what is your reaction?

PRAYER

Pray that when you are met by Christ in your life, you will have the courage and grace to respond to his call. Give thanks for all those, in many walks of life, who allow the risen Christ to guide them.

Our Father . . .

CONCLUSION

Risen Lord Jesus Christ, Son of the living God, you are the springtime of our lives; grant us the gift of joy that our hearts may sing aloud your praise, with all the saints and angels, now, and for evermore. Amen.

TUESDAY EVENING

PRESENCE AND PEACE

O Lord Jesus Christ, you are the Way, and journey with us on our pilgrimage. Be with us in the stillness of our hearts, and sustain us with your most loving presence all the days of our life, for your mercy, and for your truth's sake. Amen.

PRAISE Psalm 111.1

I will give thanks to the Lord with my whole heart,
in the company of the faithful and in the congregation.

READING Genesis 32.22-29

During the night Jacob rose, and taking his two wives, his two slave-girls, and his eleven sons, he crossed the ford of Jabbok. After he had sent them across the wadi with all that he had, Jacob was left alone, and a man wrestled with him there till daybreak. When the man saw that he could not get the better of Jacob, he struck him in the hollow of his thigh, so that Jacob's hip was dislocated as they wrestled. The man said, 'Let me go, for day is breaking,' but Jacob replied, 'I will not let you go unless you bless me.' The man asked, 'What is your name?' 'Jacob,' he answered. The man said, 'Your name shall no longer be Jacob but Israel, because you have striven with

God and with mortals, and have prevailed.' Jacob said,
'Tell me your name, I pray.' He replied, 'Why do you ask
my name?' but he gave him his blessing there.

REFLECTION

*The story of Jacob wrestling with the angel has a timeless
quality. It is full of mystery: who was the angel? Why would he
not tell Jacob what his name was? There is something terribly
unequal about all our encounters with God. God reveals as
much of himself to us as he chooses and as much as he knows
we can bear. For the rest, we have to wait in patient
faithfulness and in a cloud of unknowing.*

CONFESSION

Lord God, the darkness of my sin dislocates my life and
fractures my relationships; have mercy upon me and bring
your healing to my troubled soul, for Jesus' sake. Amen.

PRAYER

*Give thanks for all that you have learnt today of the mystery
of God. Pray for those who wrestle this night with fears and
anxieties, that they may be met by God's most loving peace.*

Our Father . . .

CONCLUSION

Lord God, at this evening hour,
rest in my heart and be to me a blessing.

WEDNESDAY MORNING

PRESENCE AND PEACE Psalm 130.4
I wait for the Lord; my soul waits for him;
in his word is my hope.

Lord Jesus Christ, risen and in our midst; let your grace
and peace enfold my life that I may be at one with you,
for your name's sake. Amen.

PRAISE Psalm 73.25
Whom have I in heaven but you?
And there is nothing upon earth that I desire
in comparison with you.

READING John 21.15-17
After breakfast Jesus said to Simon Peter, 'Simon son of
John, do you love me more than these others?' 'Yes, Lord,'
he answered, 'you know that I love you.' 'Then feed my
lambs,' he said. A second time he asked, 'Simon son of
John, do you love me?' 'Yes, Lord, you know that I love
you.' 'Then tend my sheep.' A third time he said, 'Simon
son of John, do you love me?' Peter was hurt that he
asked him a third time, 'Do you love me?' 'Lord,' he said,

'you know everything; you know I love you.' Jesus said,
'Then feed my sheep.'

REFLECTION

*This conversation between Jesus and Peter, on the face of it,
seems rather curious. It is no wonder that Peter is described as
being hurt. But if you think of it in the context of the last
days of Jesus' life on earth, when Peter denied Jesus three
times, it makes more sense. The threefold denial is followed by
the threefold affirmation. It is very moving that God seems to
take us as we are, weaknesses and all, and still use us and love
us into his purposes. What are the weaknesses that you want
to bring to God? Remember that it is our weaknesses that
God challenges and redeems out of love.*

PRAYER

*Pray for any people you feel you have not treated well and
may even have betrayed. Pray for all those people who feel
that life is grossly unjust and who have lost all trust. Pray for
Peter's humanity and courage in your dealings today.*

Our Father . . .

CONCLUSION

O Lord most mighty, you know all the secrets of our
hearts; renew, rebuild our lives that we may serve you
faithfully and proclaim the gospel of your risen presence,
now and always. Amen.

WeDNeSDAY EVENING

PRESENCE AND PEACE Psalm 117.2

For great is his steadfast love towards us,
and the faithfulness of the Lord endures for ever.

PRAISE Psalm 117.1

O praise the Lord, all you nations;
praise him, all you peoples.

READING Ruth 1.8-9,14b-17

Naomi said to her daughters-in-law, 'Go back, both of you,
home to your own mothers. May the Lord keep faith with
you, as you have kept faith with the dead and with me;
and may he grant each of you the security of a home with
a new husband.' And she kissed them goodbye. They wept
aloud . . . Orpah kissed her mother-in-law and took her
leave, but Ruth clung close to her. 'Look', said Naomi, 'your
sister-in-law has gone back to her people and her god. Go,
follow her.' Ruth answered, 'Do not urge me to go back
and desert you. Where you go, I shall go, and where you
stay, I shall stay. Your people will be my people, and your
God my God. Where you die, I shall die, and there be
buried. I solemnly declare before the Lord that nothing
but death will part me from you.'

REFLECTION

The opening verses of the book of Ruth represent the storyteller's art at its most simple and most carefully crafted. Ruth vows that where her mother-in-law goes, there she will go. The commitment in love and friendship is total. Ruth is the grandmother of the great King David. One of the powerful themes of the Old Testament, that God is in an unbreakable covenant relationship with the Chosen People, finds echoes in the story of Ruth and her devotion to her mother-in-law. The covenant of God with us is also unbreakable. We see that in Christ's life and in his promises to us. Thank God with all your heart for his faithfulness.

CONFESSION

Lord God, your love for me is boundless, yet I turn away from you, and refuse to follow your way. I repent of my sin and am truly sorry, have mercy upon me, have mercy upon me for Jesus Christ's sake. Amen.

PRAYER

Give thanks for all writers and storytellers who increase our understanding of our own humanity. Pray for all in the media, that they may live in integrity and truth. Our Father . . .

CONCLUSION

Faithful God, as you walk with me, grant me the joy of knowing your presence.

THURSDAY MORNING

PRESENCE AND PEACE Psalm 93.1
The Lord is king and has put on glorious apparel;
the Lord has put on his glory
  and girded himself with strength.

Lord of glory, let your kingly reign begin on earth, and
rule our hearts with love and truth, for Jesus' sake.

PRAISE Psalm 150.1
O praise God in his holiness;
praise him in the firmament of his power.

READING John 17.1-5
Then Jesus looked up to heaven and said:
'Father, the hour has come. Glorify your Son, that the
Son may glorify you. For you have made him sovereign
over all mankind, to give eternal life to all whom you
have given him. This is eternal life: to know you the only
true God, and Jesus Christ whom you have sent. I have
glorified you on earth by finishing the work which you
gave me to do; and now, Father, glorify me in your own
presence with the glory which I had with you before the
world began.'

REFLECTION

John often writes in a style that is very different from the other Evangelists. In this piece, which is part of the Farewell Discourses of Jesus with his disciples, Jesus' speech is meditative. The piece contains an enigmatic definition of eternal life: to know God and to know Jesus. But, actually, that definition, whilst perplexing, is true, isn't it? Our knowledge of God through Jesus is coloured by truth; all truth derives from God, and God is eternal. Therefore, to know truth is to participate in the very life of God. In what way does living in truth shape who you are and what you do?

PRAYER

Pray for all those in schools and universities who try to discover and teach what is true. Pray for yourself that you may grow in truth with each day that passes.

Our Father . . .

CONCLUSION

Christ is the morning star
who when the darkness of the world is past
brings to his saints the light of life
and opens everlasting day.
Venerable Bede (673–735)

THURSDAY evening

PRESENCE AND PEACE Psalm 59.20
To you, O my strength, will I sing;
for you, O God, are my refuge,
    my God of steadfast love.

PRAISE Psalm 75.1
We give you thanks, O God, we give you thanks,
for your name is near, as your wonderful deeds declare.

READING John 17.13-19
Now I am coming to you; but while I am still in the world
I speak these words, so that they may have my joy within
them in full measure. I have delivered your word to them,
and the world hates them because they are strangers in
the world, as I am. I do not pray you to take them out of
the world, but to keep them from the evil one. They are
strangers in the world, as I am. Consecrate them by the
truth; your word is the truth. As you sent me into the
world, I have sent them into the world, and for their sake
I consecrate myself, that they too may be consecrated by
the truth.'

REFLECTION

In these verses from the Farewell Discourses, John explores what is meant by truth. It is not only a matter of intellectual integrity but also of being in a relationship with God, and with others, marked by consecration. Would you describe your life as being consecrated by truth?

CONFESSION

Almighty and most merciful Father, forgive my lack of integrity, my waywardness, my sin. Create a new heart and a right spirit within me, that I may learn to walk in your truth all the days of my life, through Jesus Christ our Lord. Amen.

PRAYER

Pray for people who live under duress and in places where truth is not valued.

Our Father . . .

CONCLUSION

O Lord Jesus Christ,
you are the way, the truth and the life;
We pray you not to allow us to stray from you, the Way,
nor to distrust you, the Truth,
nor to rest in any other than you, the Life.
Teach us what to believe, what to do,
and in what we may take our rest.
Erasmus (1467-1536), adapted

FRIDAY MORNING

PRESENCE AND PEACE

O God, your spirit of love enfolds me, your spirit of grace upholds me; may your beauty so shine in my life that my heart, my soul and my mind become a song of praise for you, now and for ever. Amen

PRAISE Psalm 150.6

Let everything that has breath
praise the Lord.
    Alleluia.

READING Acts 2.1-4

The day of Pentecost had come, and they were all together in one place. Suddenly there came from the sky what sounded like a strong, driving wind, a noise which filled the whole house where they were sitting. And there appeared to them flames like tongues of fire distributed among them and coming to rest on each one. They were filled with the Holy Spirit and began to talk in other tongues, as the Spirit gave them power of utterance.

REFLECTION

The Spirit of God is described in these verses as being full of energy, like the power of a gale, like the force of a fire. Elsewhere in the Bible, the Spirit is described as being like a dove, or like breath. The truth that the writers are trying to convey is that God is powerful, mysterious and profoundly creative. The Spirit changes things. It's as though the Spirit creates an entirely new language and a new way of living. Our lives as Christians need always to be open to the power and the gentleness of God. We should give ourselves to him, knowing that he will shape our lives for the things that lie ahead. And ultimately, through Christ, he will recreate us in glory, in heaven.

PRAYER

Pray that the Holy Spirit may fill your life and direct you in the way you should go. Pray for the Church, and Christians throughout the world, that God may constantly renew them with the gifts of his Spirit. Give thanks for God's boundless, self-giving energy and love.

Our Father . . .

CONCLUSION

O most merciful Redeemer, friend and brother,
may I know you more clearly,
love you more dearly,
and follow you more nearly, day by day
Richard of Chichester (1197–1253)

FRIDAY EVENING

PRESENCE AND PEACE Psalm 124.7
Our help is in the name of the Lord,
who has made heaven and earth.

PRAISE Psalm 103.22
Bless the Lord, all you works of his,
    in all places of his dominion;
bless the Lord, O my soul.

READING Isaiah 11.1-3
Then a branch will grow from the stock of Jesse,
and a shoot will spring from his roots.
On him the spirit of the Lord will rest:
a spirit of wisdom and understanding,
a spirit of counsel and power,
a spirit of knowledge and fear of the Lord;
and in the fear of the Lord will be his delight.

REFLECTION
*It is easy to forget, when thinking about the Holy Spirit, that
God is, as it were, deeply personal. In other words, it is in the life,
death and resurrection of Jesus Christ that God reveals himself
to us as he truly is: wise, compassionate, challenging, self-giving,*

utterly committed to us in love, Creator, Redeemer, one who walks with us, and who longs and works for the healing of the world. Isaiah gives us a lyrical description of the Christ: one whose words are truth, who will bring justice and usher in a reign of peace. In what sense is your life part of that vision?

CONFESSION

Lord Jesus Christ, Son of God, have mercy on me, a sinner; forgive those sins that are mine alone, forgive those sins I share with all humanity, forgive those sins that prevent others from knowing you. Lord Jesus Christ, Son of God, have mercy on us all.

PRAYER

Pray that you may be made whole by the Spirit of God. Pray that your family and friends may receive the gifts of the Spirit: love, joy, peace, patience, kindness, goodness, fidelity, gentleness and self-control.

Our Father . . .

CONCLUSION

To God the Father, who loved us and made us accepted in the Beloved: to God the Son, who loved us and loosed us from our sins by his own blood: to God the Holy Spirit, who sheds the love of God abroad in our hearts: to the one true God, be all love and all glory for time and eternity. Amen. **Thomas Ken (1637–1711)**

INDEX OF AUTHORS AND SOURCES

ACKNOWLEDGEMENTS

The compiler and publisher gratefully acknowledge permission to reproduce copyright material in this anthology. Every effort has been made to trace and contact copyright holders. If there are any inadvertent omissions we apologize to those concerned; please send any information to the publisher who will make a full acknowledgement in future editions.

The Archbishops' Council: Texts from *Common Worship: Services and Prayers for the Church of England*, copyright © 2000, reproduced by permission. The Lord's Prayer in its modern form, translation prepared by the English Language Liturgical Consultation, from *Praying Together* © ELLC 1988 (p. xvi).

Darton, Longman & Todd: 'God made me' from George Appleton, *Prayers from a Troubled Heart*, 1983 (p. 31)

Oxford University Press: Bible texts from the Revised English Bible, copyright © Oxford University Press and Cambridge University Press 1989, reproduced by permission.